A DICTIONARY OF
DINOSAURS

by
Rupert Matthews

Illustrated by
Chris Forsey

MACMILLAN

Acanthopholis

Acanthopholis

(Ah-can-thoff-oll-iss)

Acanthopholis was a plant-eating dinosaur. 'Dinosaur' is the name given to a group of reptiles that lived from 225 to 65 million years ago but completely died out. There are no dinosaurs alive today. Acanthopholis was longer than a small truck and had bony plates along its back. It lived in Britain about 120 million years ago.

Albertosaurus

(Al-ber-tow-saw-rus)

Albertosaurus was a large, powerful meat-eating dinosaur that lived about 70 million years ago. It was about 9 metres long and stood twice as tall as a man and was probably able to run quickly. It most probably attacked and killed other dinosaurs for food, using its long, sharp teeth and the fierce talons on its hind legs as weapons. The scientific name for a meat-eater is a 'carnivore'. Albertosaurus means 'reptile from Alberta' and it was called this because its preserved bones – called fossils – were found in Alberta, Canada. Fossils are the bones, teeth and other remains of extinct animals which have been trapped in rock and, over millions of years, have turned to stone. Fish and plant fossils also exist.

Albertosaurus

Anatosaurus

Allosaurus

Allosaurus
(Al-owe-saw-rus)

Allosaurus lived for a long time during what fossil experts call the late Jurassic period. This was from 195 to 135 million years ago. This enormous creature – it was about 12 metres long – was a good hunter and could attack other large dinosaurs. It walked on its hind legs and was rather agile for its size. Its long, sharp teeth were serrated like steak knives and its short front legs had sharp claws that were useful for attacking prey.

Anatosaurus
(An-at-owe-saw-rus)

Anatosaurus was a duck-billed dinosaur. It had a horny beak at the front of its head. It was about 12 metres long and lived in North America 70 million years ago.

Anchisaurus
(An-kee-saw-rus)

Anchisaurus lived about 200 million years ago, earlier than most other dinosaurs. Its fossils have been found in North America and Africa. This small dinosaur, about 2 metres long, was very slim and agile, allowing it to escape from predators. Anchisaurus had short blunt teeth, which indicates that it ate plants. The scientific name for a plant-eater is a 'herbivore'. Its strong legs and sharp claws made it possible for this dinosaur to catch small animals.

Anchisaurus

Ankylosaurus

Ankylosaurus
(An-kee-low-saw-rus)

This plant-eating dinosaur was found in North America and lived about 70 million years ago. Ankylosaurus was as large as a tank and was covered in thick, bony armour, which protected it from being attacked by meat-eating dinosaurs. Even its eyelids were plated with bone! Ankylosaurus had a huge club-shaped bone at the end of its tail. Large, powerful muscles were attached to the tail to swing the tail-club around. If an Ankylosaurus were attacked, it could defend itself with its tail-club.

Apatosaurus
(Ah-pat-owe-saw-rus)

Apatosaurus was a huge, plant-eating dinosaur. It was 21 metres long and weighed up to 30 tonnes. It lived about 140 million years ago in North America. Apatosaurus used its long neck to reach the tree tops where it gathered leaves to eat. This dinosaur's tail was very long too, and ended in a thin whiplash. Scientists used to call it Brontosaurus until they realised that the Brontosaurus fossils were the same as those of the dinosaur called Apatosaurus. Since a dinosaur cannot be called by two different names, Apatosaurus was chosen.

Archaeopteryx
(Ar-kee-op-ter-icks)

Archaeopteryx was not a true dinosaur but is the earliest known bird. It lived about 150 million years ago in central Europe. Archaeopteryx had feathers and wings like a bird but teeth and a bony tail like a reptile. Its ancestors were reptiles and over many thousands of years developed into birds. Archaeopteryx was as big as a crow, and fed on small animals such as insects and lizards. This early bird's wings were quite weak, and it probably was not a good flyer. Some scientists think that Archaeopteryx was related to small dinosaurs, such as Compsognathus. If they are right, then all birds are related to the ancient dinosaurs.

Brachiosaurus

(Brack-ee-owe-saw-rus)

Brachiosaurus was so tall that it could have looked over the tops of most modern houses. It lived about 135 million years ago in East Africa. Brachiosaurus was a plant-eating dinosaur. By virtue of its long neck, Brachiosaurus could reach higher than most other animals. Its teeth were short and shaped like pegs, which is how we know that it ate leaves. Unlike most dinosaurs, Brachiosaurus had front legs that were longer than its hind legs. This gave Brachiosaurus its name, which means 'arm reptile'.

Brontosaurus

(Bron-tow-saw-rus)

Brontosaurus fossils were discovered in North America in 1879. Because of the way that its skeleton was reconstructed, it took until 1975 for the scientists to realise that Brontosaurus was the same as Apatosaurus (see opposite).

Archaeopteryx

Apatosaurus

Brachiosaurus

Cc

Camarasaurus

Camptosaurus

—— Camptosaurus ——
(Camp-tow-saw-rus)

This dinosaur could grow up to 7 metres long and was found in Europe and North America where it lived 145 million years ago. Camptosaurus walked on its hind legs most of the time, but sometimes travelled on all fours when feeding. It was one of the first plant-eating dinosaurs to have cheeks. This important development meant that it could chew its food properly before swallowing. Most successful plant-eating dinosaurs had cheeks.

—— Camarasaurus ——
(Cam-ar-ah-saw-rus)

Camarasaurus was a large plant-eating dinosaur, about 18 metres long. It ate leaves from the lower branches of trees. It had massive pillar-shaped legs that were strong enough to carry the enormous weight of the dinosaur. Camarasaurus lived about 140 million years ago in North America.

Ceratosaurus

Cetiosaurus

Cetiosaurus

(Set-ee-owe-saw-rus)

Cetiosaurus was similar in many ways to Apatosaurus. It was a large, plant-eating dinosaur and lived in Europe and Africa about 150 million years ago.

Chasmosaurus

(Chass-mow-saw-rus)

Chasmosaurus was one of the first horned dinosaurs. It lived about 80 million years ago in North America. Chasmosaurus's horns were rather small, but the frill around its neck was very big. Scientists think that horned dinosaurs such as this one only used their horns for defence, not for attacking other animals.

Ceratosaurus

(Sir-at-owe-saw-rus)

Ceratosaurus was a meat-eating dinosaur that lived in the same place as Camptosaurus. Ceratosaurus may have hunted Camptosaurus, attacking with its sharp teeth and powerful arms. It was about 6 metres long and could run quickly. It probably hunted in packs. Ceratosaurus was the only meat-eating dinosaur to have a horn on its nose. Experts do not know exactly what this was for but suspect it might have been used as a weapon or was simply just for show.

Chasmosaurus

Cc

Chialingosaurus

— Chialingosaurus —
(Chiy-al-in-go-saw-rus)

This dinosaur lived 150 million years ago in China. It was as long as a car, and was very slender. The plates on its back may have acted as protective armour.

— Coelophysis —
(See-low-fizz-is)

A small, fast hunter, Coelophysis lived in North America 210 million years ago and preyed upon lizards and smaller animals. It scampered about on its long hind legs and used its front legs to catch prey. Its mouth was full of small, needle-sharp teeth ideal for biting its food.

Coelophysis

Coelurus

— Coelurus —
(See-loo-rus)

This small dinosaur was around 1.8 metres tall. It had long legs which helped it run very quickly and catch small lizard-like animals for food. Coelurus lived about 140 million years ago in North America.

Compsognathus

Compsognathus
(Comp-sog-nay-thus)

Compsognathus is the smallest adult dinosaur ever found. It lived in Europe about 140 million years ago and was only about the size of a chicken. This tiny creature was very agile and ran quickly on its hind legs. The front legs were short with three small claws on each hand. Compsognathus may have hunted small animals in dense undergrowth, using its front legs to hold its prey. Scientists believe it might also have been a scavenger. When a large meat-eating dinosaur made a kill, Compsognathus would have snatched a mouthful of meat and then run away quickly.

Corythosaurus
(Corry-thow-saw-rus)

Up to 10 metres long – as long as three cars parked end to end, this dinosaur ate very tough plant food such as pine needles and twigs. We know that Corythosaurus ate food like this because a fossil of its stomach has been found containing pine needles and twigs. It needed a remarkable mouth to eat this food. It had a hard beak at the front, which was useful for biting twigs from trees. The teeth behind the beak were used to chew on tough food. Corythosaurus had hundreds of teeth, arranged in long rows on both sides of its mouth. Each tooth was ridged and able to crush the hardest foods. This made Corythosaurus a very successful dinosaur. It survived in North America from about 90 million years ago until 70 million years ago.

Corythosaurus

Dd

— Daspletosaurus —
(Daz-plet-owe-saw-rus)

The name Daspletosaurus means 'frightful reptile', which is a very good description of this ancient reptile. A relative of Tyrannosaurus, it preyed upon other dinosaurs. Daspletosaurus grew up to 9 metres long and lived 70 million years ago in North America.

Daspletosaurus

Deinonychus

— Deinonychus —
(Day-non-ee-kus)

Deinonychus was a fast-running hunter that lived about 120 million years ago in North America. It was around 3 metres long and was probably the most dangerous meat-eating dinosaur of its time. When it attacked other dinosaurs, Deinonychus used the two large, sharp, curved claws on its hind feet. Scientists think the Deinonychus may have balanced on one hind foot, while it slashed its prey to death with the claw on the other. Then it used its big teeth to tear off lumps of meat.

— Dicraeosaurus —
(Dye-cray-owe-saw-rus)

Dicraeosaurus was what scientists call a sauropod dinosaur – one that ate plants, had a small head and long neck and tail, and had five-toed limbs. It lived in Africa during the Jurassic period 195 to 135 million years ago. Dicraeosaurus grew to 13 metres long.

Dicraeosaurus

Dilophosaurus

Dilophosaurus
(Dill-off-owe-saw-rus)

Dilophosaurus was a large meat-eater that lived 180 million years ago. It was a very unusual dinosaur as it had two thin crests of bone on top of its skull. These crests were very fragile, and probably would have broken if used as weapons. Some scientists think that the crests may have been used to signal to other Dilophosauruses in the same manner that peacocks signal to each other with their tails.

Dimorphodon

Dimorphodon
(Dye-morf-owe-don)

Dimorphodon was a very early flying reptile. These flying animals are not really dinosaurs, but are called 'pterosaurs'. Dimorphodon lived about 180 million years ago in Britain. With its long legs, and a tail that was used for balance, this flyer might also have been a good runner.

Diplodocus
(Dip-lod-owe-cus)

With a length of 27 metres, Diplodocus was one of the longest dinosaurs known. This is about as long as eight cars parked end to end! However, it was not one of the heaviest dinosaurs but was rather slim. Most of its length was made up by its thin neck and tail. Diplodocus ate plants, and used its long neck to reach leaves in the tops of tall trees, just as a giraffe does today. It lived in North America about 140 million years ago.

Diplodocus

Dd

Dromaeosaurus
(Drom-ee-owe-saw-rus)

This dinosaur was about 1.8 metres tall – the same height as a man. It was a ferocious, fast-running hunter and probably attacked dinosaurs about the same size as itself, such as Dromiceiomimus. It may also have eaten small creatures such as lizards and mammals. The sharp claws on its hind legs were used to slash at large prey. Dromaeosaurus ran on its hind legs, holding its tail stiffly, which helped to balance the weight of its body.

Dromiceiomimus
(Drom-iss-ee-owe-my-mus)

Dromiceiomimus was one of the fast-running creatures called 'ostrich dinosaurs'. As you can see from the picture, it was the shape of an ostrich and had a tail. Dromiceiomimus measured 3-4 metres from head to tail tip, and lived about 70 million years ago in Canada. It was able to run as fast as a modern horse and may have been the swiftest of all dinosaurs. Well-built for speed, the hind legs were long, slender, and powered by immensely strong muscles. The whole body was very light. Dromiceiomimus could escape its enemies by running away at high speed.

Dromaeosaurus

Dromiceiomimus

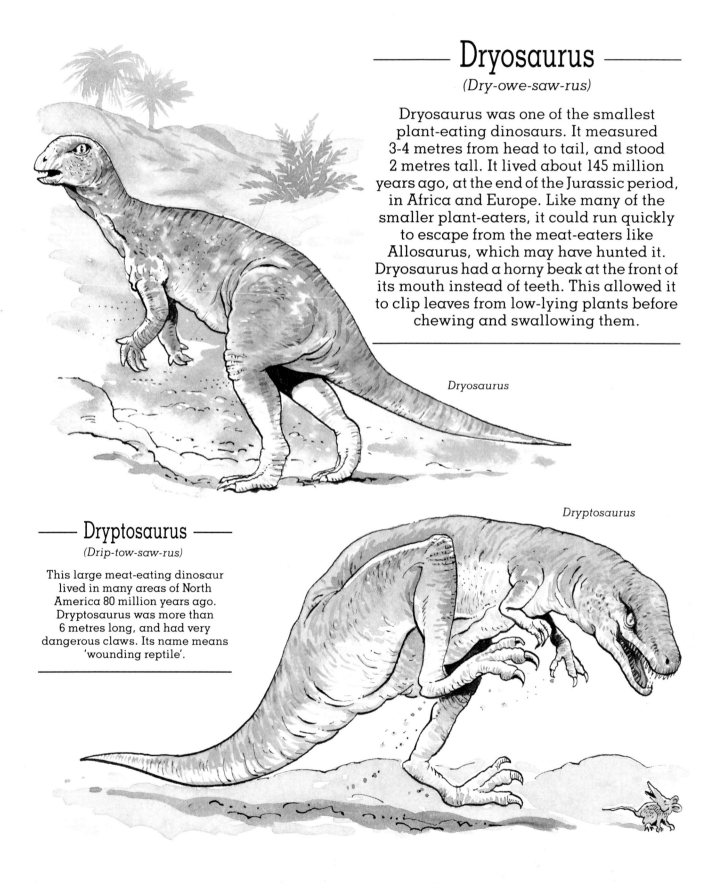

Dryosaurus
(Dry-owe-saw-rus)

Dryosaurus was one of the smallest plant-eating dinosaurs. It measured 3-4 metres from head to tail, and stood 2 metres tall. It lived about 145 million years ago, at the end of the Jurassic period, in Africa and Europe. Like many of the smaller plant-eaters, it could run quickly to escape from the meat-eaters like Allosaurus, which may have hunted it. Dryosaurus had a horny beak at the front of its mouth instead of teeth. This allowed it to clip leaves from low-lying plants before chewing and swallowing them.

Dryosaurus

Dryptosaurus

Dryptosaurus
(Drip-tow-saw-rus)

This large meat-eating dinosaur lived in many areas of North America 80 million years ago. Dryptosaurus was more than 6 metres long, and had very dangerous claws. Its name means 'wounding reptile'.

Edmontosaurus

— Edmontosaurus —

(Ed-mon-tow-saw-rus)

This was a duck-billed dinosaur like Anatosaurus. Edmontosaurus was among the largest duck-bills, and grew up to 13 metres tall. It lived at the end of the Cretaceous period, 136 to 65 million years ago, and was one of the last dinosaurs to exist.

Elaphrosaurus

— Elaphrosaurus —

(Ell-aff-row-saw-rus)

Elaphrosaurus was the earliest of the 'ostrich dinosaurs'. It lived about 150 million years ago and may have been the ancestor of the ostrich dinosaurs, such as Dromiceiomimus and Struthiomimus. It had shorter legs than other ostrich dinosaurs and probably could not run as fast.

— Elasmosaurus —

(Ell-as-mow-saw-rus)

Elasmosaurus was a large reptile that lived in the shallow seas that covered part of North America about 80 million years ago. It was not a dinosaur – these all lived on land – but belonged to a different group of reptiles. Elasmosaurus had a very long neck which could move quickly in almost any direction. At the end of the neck was a small head with a mouth full of long, sharp teeth – ideal for catching fish. Some scientists think that Elasmosaurus might also have been able to catch pterodactyls (see entry) as they flew low over the sea.

Elasmosaurus

—— Euskelosaurus ——

(You-skel-owe-saw-rus)

This large, plant-eating dinosaur lived at the end of the Triassic period (about 210 million years ago) in South Africa. The very first dinosaurs lived during this period.

—— Fabrosaurus ——

(Fab-row-saw-rus)

This small creature was one of the very first ornithischian, or bird-hipped, dinosaurs. Fabrosaurus was only about 1 metre tall and walked on its hind legs. It could run away from danger quite quickly. Like all other dinosaurs in this group, Fabrosaurus ate plants. It had lots of teeth shaped to grind up tough plant food. Fabrosaurus lived in South Africa about 210 million years ago.

Euskelosaurus

Fabrosaurus

— Gallimimus —
(Gal-ee-my-mus)

Gallimimus lived 65 million years ago in central Asia. It was similar to Struthiomimus (see entry) but was larger. Gallimimus grew up to about 5 metres long, and was a powerful runner.

Gallimimus

Heterodontosaurus

— Heterodontosaurus —
(Heta-row-don-tow-saw-rus)

This name means 'reptile with different teeth' and this is what makes Heterodontosaurus very unusual. Most dinosaurs only had one type of tooth in their mouths but Heterodontosaurus had sharp, nipping teeth at the front of its mouth, a pair of tusks halfway along each jaw, and flat, grinding teeth at the back of the mouth. This small dinosaur ate plants and lived in South Africa about 220 million years ago.

Hylaeosaurus
(Hi-lay-owe-saw-rus)

Covered with thick, bony armour which had sharp spikes and thick knobs, this strange dinosaur roamed Britain during the early Cretaceous period. The experts have so far only been able to guess at what a Hylaeosaurus really looked like. This is because the skeleton that was found is still set in a block of stone.

Hypsilophodon
(Hip-sill-off-owe-don)

Hypsilophodon was more than 2 metres tall, and lived 130 million years ago in Britain and Europe. Its name means 'high ridged tooth'. In fact, it is fossils of the teeth of this dinosaur which are found most often. Hypsilophodon ate plants and could run quite quickly on its hind legs, using its tail to aid balance.

Hylaeosaurus

Hypsilophodon

Ichthyosaurus

Ichthyosaurus

(Ick-thee-owe-saw-rus)

This reptile looked like a dolphin and was superbly adapted to living in the sea. It could swim very quickly indeed and used its powerful tail to push itself through the water, steering with its flippers. Scientists think that it lived on a diet of fish and squid. Ichthyosaurus was different from most reptiles as it did not lay eggs. Instead, the mother kept her eggs in her body until they were ready to hatch and then gave birth to live young. Ichthyosaurus means 'fish lizard'. There were many different ichthyosaurs in their family group and they lived from 210 to 80 million years ago.

Iguanodon

Iguanodon

(Ig-you-ah-no-don)

Iguanodon is one of the best-known dinosaurs. It was one of the first discovered by scientists. Over the years dozens of Iguanodon fossils have been found across Europe, Africa and Asia. Iguanodon was a large, two-legged dinosaur that ate plants. It was 10 metres long and lived about 120 million years ago. When eating, Iguanodon used its long tongue to pull plants into its mouth. It moved on its hind legs when escaping from a meat-eating dinosaur or when eating from trees. Iguanodon had large, sharp spikes on its thumbs which scientists think may have been used as weapons.

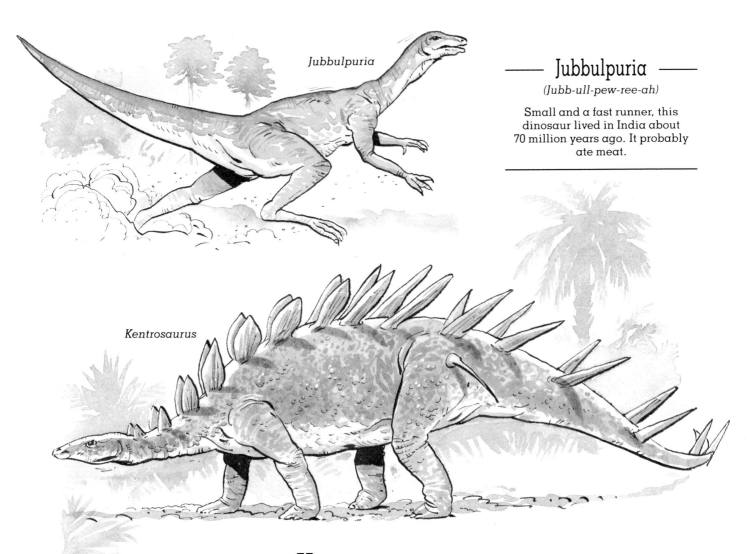

Jubbulpuria

Jubbulpuria
(Jubb-ull-pew-ree-ah)

Small and a fast runner, this dinosaur lived in India about 70 million years ago. It probably ate meat.

Kentrosaurus

Kentrosaurus
(Ken-trow-saw-rus)

This armour-plated dinosaur was 2.5 metres long and lived about 145 million years ago in Africa. It moved slowly – in fact, you could probably run faster than a Kentrosaurus!
It plodded around munching low-growing plants, such as ferns. Kentrosaurus had impressive spikes and plates along its back which probably helped to protect it from large meat-eating dinosaurs. Scientists think that the plates were covered with skin. If Kentrosaurus became too hot it could stand sideways in a breeze. This would have cooled the blood in the skin over the plates. Also if Kentrosaurus became too cool it could turn its plates to face the sun and get warm.

Lambeosaurus

Lambeosaurus

(Lam-be-owe-saw-rus)

This huge duck-billed dinosaur was nearly 15 metres long and had a large, curiously shaped crest on its head. Inside the crest was a large hollow space, connected to the dinosaur's nostrils. Some scientists think that Lambeosaurus would have used this to make noises to call to other dinosaurs. Lambeosaurus fossils have been found with crests bigger than the skull. This dinosaur lived in North America about 70 million years ago.

Leptoceratops
(Lep-tow-sir-ah-tops)

This small dinosaur was shorter than a man. It was a member of the horned dinosaur family, but it had no horns and only a very small frill around its neck! Most horned dinosaurs were large and walked on all fours, but Leptoceratops was able to run quickly on its hind legs. This strange creature lived 70 million years ago in North America.

Leptoceratops

Lufengosaurus

Lufengosaurus
(Lu-fen-go-saw-rus)

This early dinosaur was given its name because its fossils were found near Lufeng in China. It was a large plant-eater and looked very much like another dinosaur called Plateosaurus. They were probably close relatives, as they both belonged to the same family group.

Mm

Maiasaura

(May-ah-saw-rah)

When the fossils of this dinosaur were discovered in 1978, scientists became very excited. This was because they had found a fossilised nesting site. Maiasaura itself was a very ordinary duck-billed dinosaur about 9 metres long. The female Maiasaura dug a round nest and laid her eggs in it. She then stayed near the nest until the young hatched. The young stayed in the nest while the mother Maiasaura brought food back to the nest for them to eat. Fossils show that the Maiasaura nested in large colonies of several adults and their young. This important find proved that dinosaurs looked after their young. Maiasaura lived in North America about 70 million years ago.

Maiasaura

Mamenchisaurus

(Mam-en-key-saw-rus)

This extraordinary dinosaur had the longest neck of any animal. The neck measured 10 metres long and made up almost half the total length of this large plant-eater. Mamenchisaurus lived 140 million years ago in China.

Mamenchisaurus

Megalosaurus

(Meg-al-owe-saw-rus)

Megalosaurus fossils were the first to be recognised as bones belonging to a large, extinct reptile. The fossils were studied in Britain in 1824 by William Buckland. Megalosaurus means 'big lizard'. It was a large, powerful meat-eating dinosaur that lived in Europe about 140 million years ago.

Megalosaurus

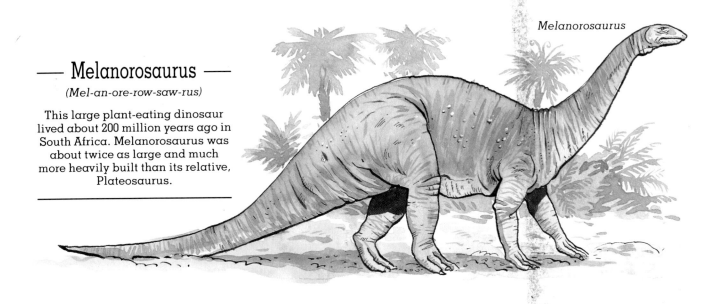

Melanorosaurus

— Melanorosaurus —

(Mel-an-ore-row-saw-rus)

This large plant-eating dinosaur lived about 200 million years ago in South Africa. Melanorosaurus was about twice as large and much more heavily built than its relative, Plateosaurus.

— Metriorhynchus —

(Met-ree-ore-ring-cus)

In the middle of the Jurassic period, about 160 million years ago, a group of crocodiles lived in the sea. The best-known of these was Metriorhynchus. This crocodile was 2.5 metres long and was well adapted to swimming. Its body was smooth and streamlined so that it could glide through the water. The long tail was powered by strong muscles and ended in a broad pair of fins. Each leg was a sturdy paddle. Metriorhynchus fed on fish, which it caught with its sharp teeth.

Metriorhynchus

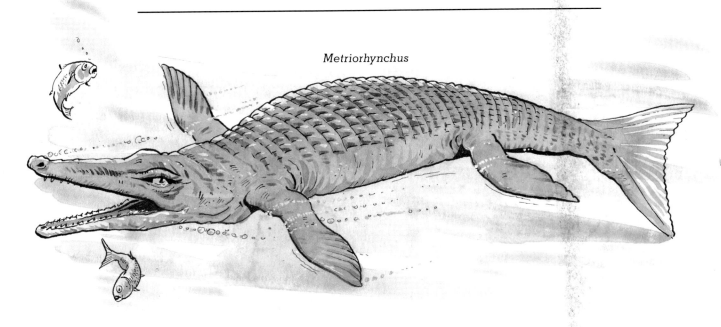

Mm

Monoclonius

(Mon-owe-clow-nee-us)

Monoclonius was a horned dinosaur about 6 metres long. It had a single horn, which grew from its nose, and a bony frill, which extended over its neck. Monoclonius lived about 74 million years ago in North America.

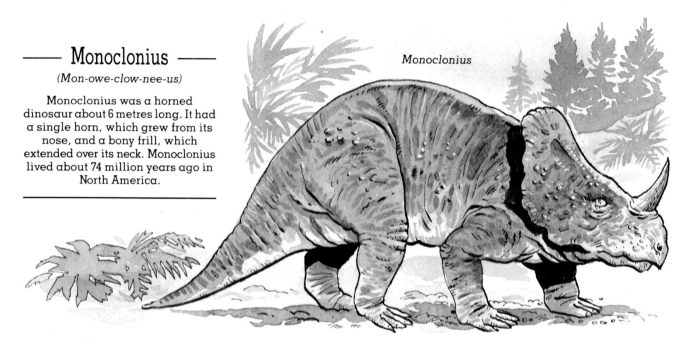

Monoclonius

Morganucodon

(Mor-ga-new-co-don)

Unlike dinosaurs, which were reptiles, Morganucodon was one of the first mammals, which lived about 200 million years ago. Today, most of the largest animals, including people, are mammals. The only mammals alive at the same time as the dinosaurs were small animals such as Morganucodon. Scientists have found the fossils of several other mammals that lived alongside the dinosaurs. They were all small, furry creatures that looked like rats. These early mammals probably hunted insects or small lizards, perhaps at night-time. The mammals took over after the dinosaurs had died out.

Morganucodon

Mosasaurus

(Mows-ah-saw-rus)

During the Cretaceous period (135 to 65 million years ago) a group of lizards, known as mosasaurs, lived in the sea and many members of this group grew to be as large as modern whales. Mosasaurus had a long, thin body which it swished from side to side to move through the water. Its long tail was flat to help it swim efficiently. The four legs were shaped like paddles and helped to steer the animal. Mosasaurus had a mouth full of sharp, round teeth. These were very strong and were ideal for biting its prey — shell-covered animals called ammonites which are now also extinct.

Mosasaurus

Muttaburrasaurus

Muttaburrasaurus

(Mut-ter-burr-ah-saw-rus)

This dinosaur's name means 'reptile from Muttaburra'. Its fossils were found near the town of Muttaburra in Australia. Muttaburrasaurus was 7 metres long and stood twice as tall as a man. It had sharp teeth with which to slice up its food. Scientists think that it may have eaten some meat, as well as plants. This makes it different from the dinosaurs to which it is related, such as Iguanodon and Ouranosaurus, which only ate plants. Muttaburrasaurus lived 100 million years ago.

Nodosaurus

(Nod-owe-saw-rus)

Nodosaurus was an armoured dinosaur that lived in North America about 95 million years ago. The nodules of armour on its body gave it its name. Unlike most armoured dinosaurs, Nodosaurus had no spikes or tail-club.

Nodosaurus

Opisthocoelicaudia

(Oh-pis-thow-see-lic-ord-ee-ah)

Opisthocoelicaudia was an unusual sauropod dinosaur. Its tail was so strong that scientists think it was used as a support when the dinosaur reared up on its hind legs. In this way, the creature could reach high into trees. This dinosaur was 12 metres long and lived 70 million years ago in central Asia.

Ornithomimus

(Ore-nith-owe-my-mus)

Slightly taller than a man, this dinosaur lived 70 million years ago in North America. Like all ostrich dinosaurs, Ornithomimus had no teeth. Instead, it had a tough, horny beak that was similar to that of a modern bird. It could run away from danger very quickly.

Ornithomimus

Opisthocoelicaudia

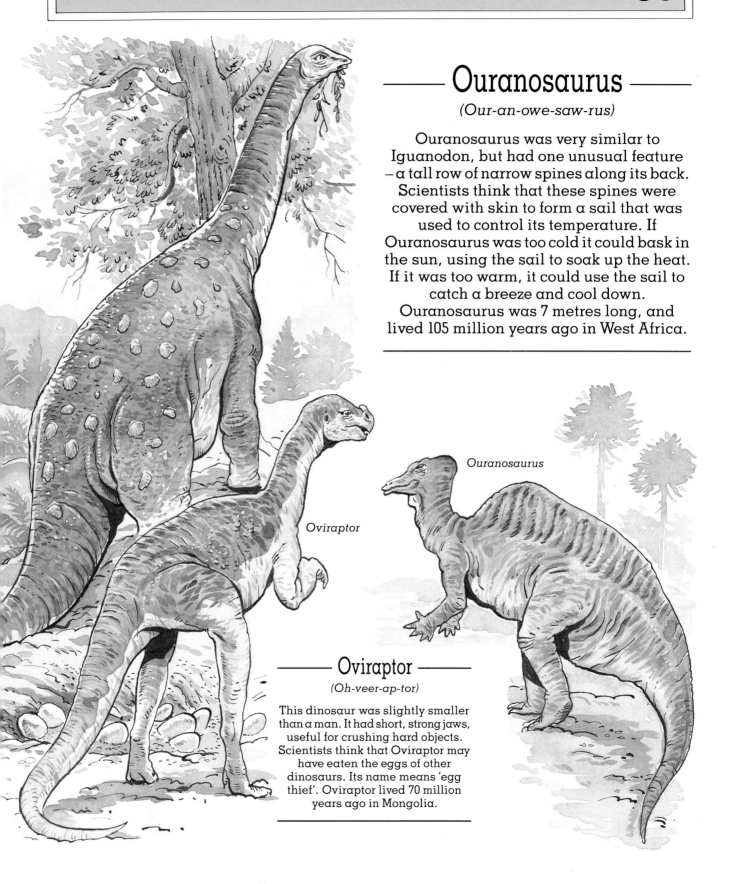

Ouranosaurus
(Our-an-owe-saw-rus)

Ouranosaurus was very similar to Iguanodon, but had one unusual feature – a tall row of narrow spines along its back. Scientists think that these spines were covered with skin to form a sail that was used to control its temperature. If Ouranosaurus was too cold it could bask in the sun, using the sail to soak up the heat. If it was too warm, it could use the sail to catch a breeze and cool down. Ouranosaurus was 7 metres long, and lived 105 million years ago in West Africa.

Ouranosaurus

Oviraptor

Oviraptor
(Oh-veer-ap-tor)

This dinosaur was slightly smaller than a man. It had short, strong jaws, useful for crushing hard objects. Scientists think that Oviraptor may have eaten the eggs of other dinosaurs. Its name means 'egg thief'. Oviraptor lived 70 million years ago in Mongolia.

Pp

Pachycephalosaurus
(Pack-ee-sef-al-owe-saw-rus)

This dinosaur's name means 'reptile with a thick head'. In fact, the bone on the top of its skull was 25 cm thick. Scientists think that Pachycephalosaurus may have used its thick skull in head-butting contests! Two rival dinosaurs would have run towards each other with their heads down. When the dinosaurs hit each other, the thick skull would have acted like a crash helmet. Pachycephalosaurus was 8 metres long, ate plants, and lived in North America about 70 million years ago, during the late Cretaceous period.

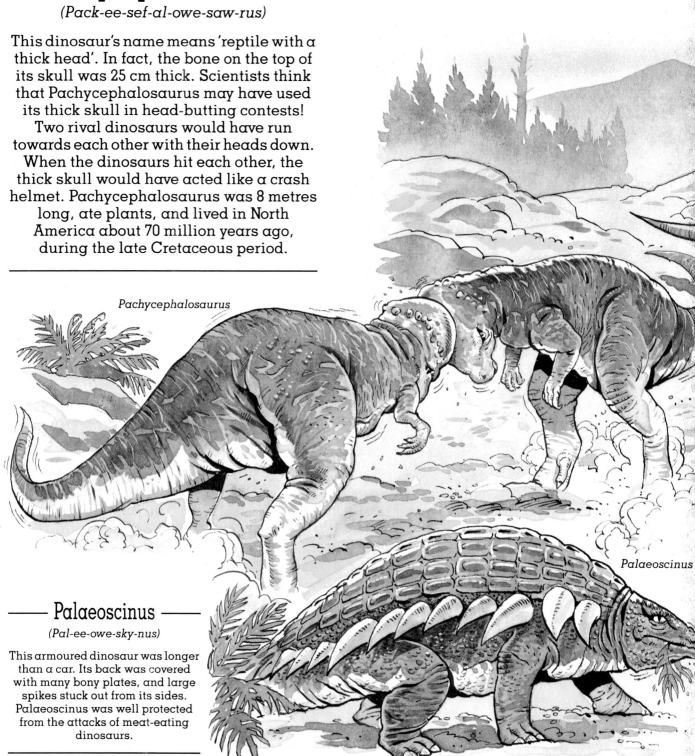

Pachycephalosaurus

Palaeoscinus

Palaeoscinus
(Pal-ee-owe-sky-nus)

This armoured dinosaur was longer than a car. Its back was covered with many bony plates, and large spikes stuck out from its sides. Palaeoscinus was well protected from the attacks of meat-eating dinosaurs.

Parasaurolophus

— Parasaurolophus —
(Par-ah-saw-rol-owe-fus)

Like other duck-billed dinosaurs, Parasaurolophus had a long bony crest on top of its head. However, this creature's crest was one of the largest. It stuck out for more than 1 metre behind the skull. The crest was hollow and contained air tubes running from the nostrils to the lungs. Some scientists think that the dinosaurs used them to make loud bellowing noises while others believe that the long air passages gave these dinosaurs a good sense of smell. Another idea is that the crests may have been brightly coloured and used for display signals.

— Phobosuchus —
(Fow-bow-such-us)

The Cretaceous period (135 to 65 million years ago) saw the appearance of the first modern crocodiles. One of these, Phobosuchus, was larger than many dinosaurs. It was four times as long as the largest modern crocodile and it was a fearsome predator which would have attacked and eaten dinosaurs.

Phobosuchus

Pinacosaurus

— Pinacosaurus —
(Pee-nah-co-saw-rus)

This armoured dinosaur lived about 80 million years ago in Mongolia. Like Ankylosaurus, Pinacosaurus had a club of bone at the end of its tail with which to defend itself.

Pp

Placodus

Placodus

(Plac-oh-dus)

Placodus was not a dinosaur, but a reptile that lived in the sea. It was able to swim well with its powerful tail and had tough, bony armour on its back. It had forward-pointing teeth at the front of its mouth which it used to pluck shellfish from rocks on the seabed, and large, flat teeth at the back of its mouth with which to crush them. Placodus lived in Europe during the late Triassic period, 225 to 195 million years ago.

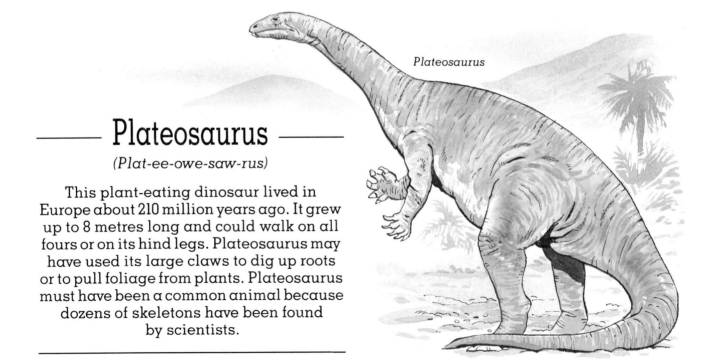

Plateosaurus

Plateosaurus

(Plat-ee-owe-saw-rus)

This plant-eating dinosaur lived in Europe about 210 million years ago. It grew up to 8 metres long and could walk on all fours or on its hind legs. Plateosaurus may have used its large claws to dig up roots or to pull foliage from plants. Plateosaurus must have been a common animal because dozens of skeletons have been found by scientists.

Pliosaurus

Plesiosaurus

Plesiosaurus

(Plea-see-owe-saw-rus)

There are many different plesiosaurs but they were all very similar. From the picture you can see that Plesiosaurus had a broad body, a short tail and a long neck. Plesiosaurs used their broad flippers to push themselves through the water. They could not swim quickly, but were very agile. A plesiosaur could change direction suddenly, and the long neck could be swiftly pointed in different directions. Scientists think that a plesiosaur swam on the surface of the sea hunting for fish. When it found some fish, it would dart its head towards them and snap them up in its mouth. Though they were reptiles, plesiosaurs were not dinosaurs.

Pliosaurus

(Plea-owe-saw-rus)

Pliosaurs were descended from early types of plesiosaur. The bodies of the two types of reptiles were very similar, but pliosaurs had short necks and large heads, like Pliosaurus, shown above. Pliosaurs could swim much more quickly than plesiosaurs. They used their strong flippers to power themselves through the water. We think pliosaurs ate creatures called cephalopods, which looked like squids with shells. Like plesiosaurs, pliosaurs died out towards the end of the Cretaceous period, about 65 million years ago.

Pp

Protoceratops

Protoceratops

(Pro-tow-sir-ah-tops)

This small dinosaur was not much larger than a big dog. It lived 80 million years ago in Mongolia and was one of the first horned dinosaurs. As you can see from the picture, it did not actually have any horns, but its large neck frill and other features put it in the same family as Triceratops and Monoclonius. Scientists have found many Protoceratops fossils in Mongolia, some of which were the remains of babies and young animals. These fossils have enabled scientists to study the way in which dinosaurs grew from eggs to adults.

Psittacosaurus

Psittacosaurus

(Sit-ah-co-saw-rus)

Psittacosaurus lived about 95 million years ago in Central Asia. It might have been the ancestor of all the later horned dinosaurs. It was a small creature – only about 2 metres long. Psittacosaurus walked mainly on its hind legs, although it could also use its front legs. It had a sharp, parrot-like beak with which it could nip leaves from bushes. The back of its skull had a small frill which became bigger in later horned dinosaurs.

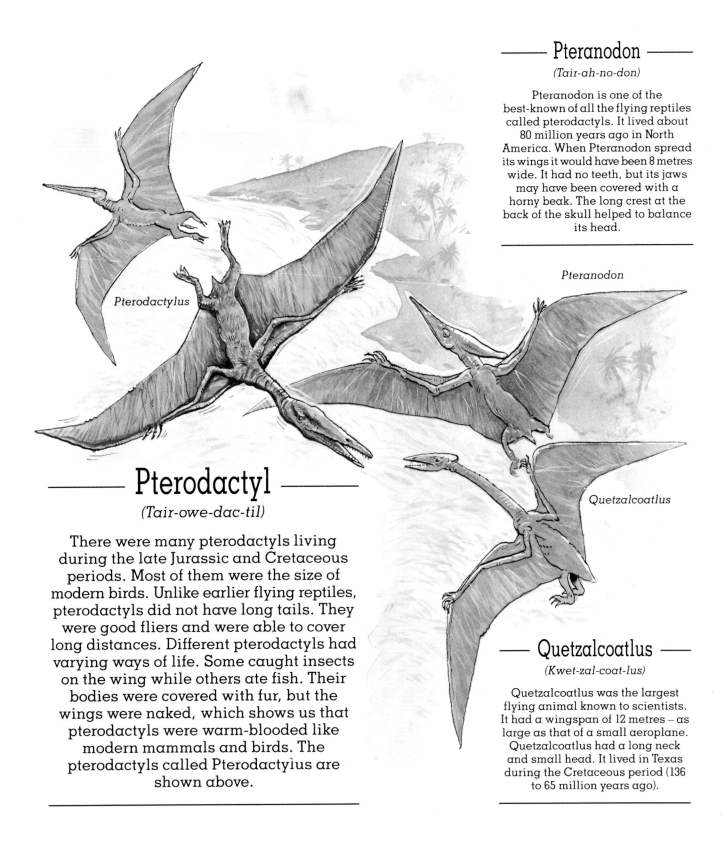

Pteranodon
(Tair-ah-no-don)

Pteranodon is one of the best-known of all the flying reptiles called pterodactyls. It lived about 80 million years ago in North America. When Pteranodon spread its wings it would have been 8 metres wide. It had no teeth, but its jaws may have been covered with a horny beak. The long crest at the back of the skull helped to balance its head.

Pteranodon

Pterodactylus

Quetzalcoatlus

Pterodactyl
(Tair-owe-dac-til)

There were many pterodactyls living during the late Jurassic and Cretaceous periods. Most of them were the size of modern birds. Unlike earlier flying reptiles, pterodactyls did not have long tails. They were good fliers and were able to cover long distances. Different pterodactyls had varying ways of life. Some caught insects on the wing while others ate fish. Their bodies were covered with fur, but the wings were naked, which shows us that pterodactyls were warm-blooded like modern mammals and birds. The pterodactyls called Pterodactylus are shown above.

Quetzalcoatlus
(Kwet-zal-coat-lus)

Quetzalcoatlus was the largest flying animal known to scientists. It had a wingspan of 12 metres – as large as that of a small aeroplane. Quetzalcoatlus had a long neck and small head. It lived in Texas during the Cretaceous period (136 to 65 million years ago).

Rhamphorhynchus

— Rhamphorhynchus —
(Ram-for-ring-cus)

During the Jurassic period the air was ruled by various types of Rhamphorhynchus. Its name means 'narrow beak'. Like pterodactyls, these flying reptiles had bodies which were covered with fur. They had long, bony tails which ended in a flap of skin. This may have been used as a rudder to steer it when flying.

Saltasaurus

— Saltasaurus —
(Salt-ah-saw-rus)

Saltasaurus was 12 metres long and nearly twice as tall as a man when measured to its shoulder. It lived about 65 million years ago and was one of the very last dinosaurs. The fossils of this dinosaur were found in the Salta province, an area of Argentina. This was a rare find as it was covered with thousands of pieces of bony armour.

Saltopus

— Saltopus —
(Salt-owe-pus)

This was an early dinosaur that lived 200 million years ago in Scotland. Saltopus was about the same size as a modern cat and may have lived in a similar way. Scientists think that Saltopus ate small lizards and mammals.

Saurolophus

Saurolophus
(Saw-rol-owe-fus)

Saurolophus lived 65 million years ago and was a plant-eating, duck-billed dinosaur which would have stood about 2 metres tall. Fossil remains have been found in both North America and Eastern Asia. It had a much smaller crest than some of the other duck-billed dinosaurs such as Parasaurolophus and Corythosaurus. Saurolophus had a typical duck-billed dinosaur's body, with webbed fingers and a powerful tail. These would have made Saurolophus a good swimmer. It may have escaped from meat-eating dinosaurs by swimming into deep water.

Saurornithoides

Saurornithoides
(Saw-ror-nith-oy-dees)

With its long legs, Saurornithoides was obviously a fast runner. It had a fourth claw on each hind foot, which was probably held clear of the ground and may have been used to attack other animals. Its hands had three claws that could have been used to hold small pieces of food. This dinosaur had very large eyes which would have been useful when hunting at dusk. For a dinosaur of its size – it was about 2 metres tall – it had a surprisingly large brain. Saurornithoides lived about 80 million years ago and was found in Mongolia.

—— Scelidosaurus ——
(Skel-id-owe-saw-rus)

This early ornithischian (bird-hipped) plant-eater lived in England about 180 million years ago. In some ways it resembled armoured dinosaurs such as Ankylosaurus, but it was also similar to plated dinosaurs such as Stegosaurus. Some scientists think that Scelidosaurus was the ancestor of both groups of dinosaurs while others put Scelidosaurus in a group of its own. It grew to 4 metres long, was rather heavy, and walked slowly on all four legs. Rows of bony knobs ran along its body and offered protection against attack from meat-eating dinosaurs.

Scelidosaurus

Scutellosaurus

—— Scutellosaurus ——
(Skut-ell-owe-saw-rus)

Scutellosaurus lived in North America nearly 200 million years ago. It walked on all fours most of the time, but could also run on its hind legs. Scutellosaurus had a very long tail and its back was covered with many protective bony plates.

—— Segisaurus ——
(Seg-ee-saw-rus)

Only slightly bigger than a turkey, this small, fast-running dinosaur lived 185 million years ago in North America. It probably ate lizards and large insects. The fossils of Segisaurus puzzle scientists because some of the bones are very unusual.

Segisaurus

—— Silvisaurus ——
(Sill-vee-saw-rus)

Another of the armoured dinosaurs, Silvisaurus was 4 metres long and it lived 95 million years ago in North America. Its back was covered with flat plates of bone which joined together into a solid shield. Sharp spines stuck out sideways from the shoulders and the end of its tail.

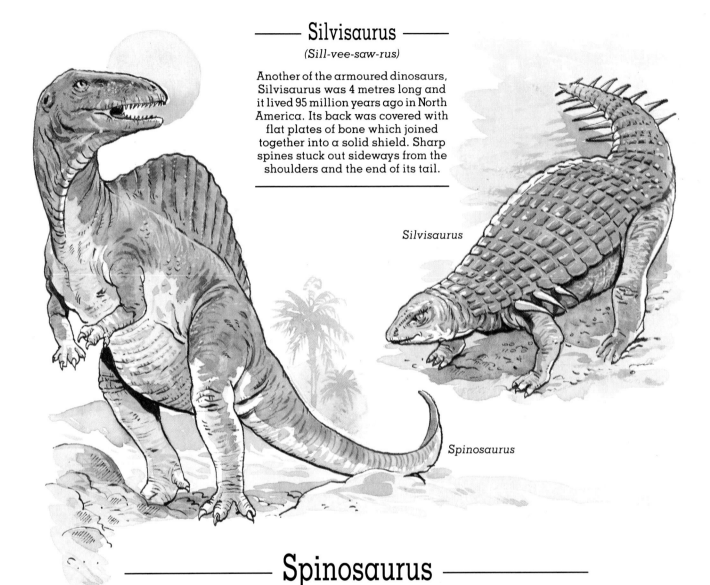

Silvisaurus

Spinosaurus

—— Spinosaurus ——
(Spy-no-saw-rus)

Fossil remains of this dinosaur were found in Egypt. It was a large meat-eater and was 12 metres long. It had a long row of spines along its back joined together by a flap of skin. The largest of these spines was taller than a man. The skin made a large sail that could have broken easily. This means Spinosaurus was unlikely to have hunted large animals. It probably scavenged meat from dinosaurs that had already died or that had been killed by other meat-eaters. Spinosaurus probably used its sail in the same way as Ouranosaurus. It lived 110 million years ago.

Staurikosaurus

— Staurikosaurus —

(Stor-rick-owe-saw-rus)

This was one of the earliest dinosaurs ever to have roamed the Earth. It was small – only 2 metres from tip to toe – but could run quickly on its hind legs. The front legs were rather short, which shows that Staurikosaurus probably used them for grasping food rather than walking. It had sharp teeth, which means that it probably ate meat. Scientists are not sure whether Staurikosaurus was related to small meat-eaters such as Saltopus or to plant-eaters like Plateosaurus. It lived during the Triassic period in South America.

— Stegoceras —

(Steg-oss-err-as)

Stegoceras was a bone-headed dinosaur, like Pachycephalosaurus. It was one of the smaller members of this group, being only 2 metres long. It would have fought other Stegoceras by head-butting, using its thick skull to take the force of the impact. Stegoceras lived 75 million years ago in China.

Stegoceras

Stegosaurus

Stegosaurus
(Steg-owe-saw-rus)

Probably the largest plated dinosaur, Stegosaurus was twice as tall as a man and grew up to 7.5 metres long. Two rows of bony plates ran along the back of this dinosaur. They were probably used to control its body heat. The sharp spines on Stegosaurus's tail would have been used against any attacking meat-eating dinosaur. This plant-eating dinosaur lived in North America 140 million years ago.

Stenonychosaurus
(Sten-on-ick-owe-saw-rus)

Stenonychosaurus was closely related to Saurornithoides, but it was even 'brainier'. In proportion to its body weight, Stenonychosaurus had a larger brain than any other dinosaur. Stenonychosaurus lived about 80 million years ago in North America.

Struthiomimus

Stenonychosaurus

Struthiomimus
(Strew-thee-owe-my-mus)

The name Struthiomimus means 'ostrich mimic'. It looked like an ostrich without feathers and was able to run very quickly. It had a compact body, long neck, a toothless mouth and long legs. It lived 75 million years ago in North America.

Styracosaurus
(Sty-rack-owe-saw-rus)

Styracosaurus was a medium-sized, horned dinosaur that lived about 80 million years ago. Styracosaurus had a single horn on its nose and a number of other spines growing from its neck frill.

Styracosaurus

Tarbosaurus

Tarbosaurus
(Tar-bow-saw-rus)

Tarbosaurus was a huge, meat-eating dinosaur. It was 14 metres long and must have been a very powerful dinosaur. One strange feature was the size of its arms, which were tiny compared to the rest of the animal. Some scientists think that they helped Tarbosaurus to stand up. When lying down on its stomach, Tarbosaurus would dig its arms into the ground to use as levers. By pushing with its hind legs, Tarbosaurus would then be able to stand up.

Tenontosaurus
(Ten-on-tow-saw-rus)

The most remarkable feature of this plant-eating dinosaur was its long tail. The tail might have been a useful defence against its enemies. Tenontosaurus lived 110 million years ago in North America.

Tenontosaurus

Thecodontosaurus

Thecodontosaurus
(Thee-co-don-tow-saw-rus)

Thecodontosaurus was an early plant-eating dinosaur. It was about the size of a large dog. Thecodontosaurus lived in Britain about 205 million years ago.

Thescelosaurus

— Thescelosaurus —

(Thess-kel-owe-saw-rus)

Thescelosaurus lived in North America about 65 million years ago, just before all the dinosaurs died out. It was a plant-eater and stood as tall as a man. Thescelosaurus may have escaped from attackers by running away quickly on its hind legs, but it also had bony studs set into its skin for protection.

Torosaurus

— Torosaurus —

(Tor-row-saw-rus)

This huge, horned dinosaur lived 65 million years ago, right at the end of the Mesozoic era. Like all horned dinosaurs, Torosaurus was a plant-eater. Its horns were used both to defend itself from meat-eating dinosaurs and to fight rival Torosaurus. The bony neck-frill was a base for its powerful jaw muscles. At over 2.5 metres long, Torosaurus's skull is larger than that of any other known land animal.

Tyrannosaurus

Triceratops

—— Triceratops ——
(Tri-sir-ah-tops)

Triceratops was a large, horned dinosaur that lived in North America. At 9 metres long and weighing up to 5.4 tonnes, it was about the size of a small truck. It lived about 65 million years ago during the Cretaceous period. Triceratops ate plants, biting the leaves with its sharp teeth. It had three large horns on its head which were useful protection from the large meat-eating dinosaurs of the time.

—— Tyrannosaurus ——
(Tie-ran-owe-saw-rus)

Tyrannosaurus was the biggest meat-eating dinosaur of all time. It was about 14 metres long and stood over 5 metres high. You can see that Tyrannosaurus had powerful claws on its hind legs. It may have used these to fight other dinosaurs and to kill them for food. Tyrannosaurus's teeth were the size of a human hand. Some scientists think that Tyrannosaurus fed on the bodies of dead dinosaurs, as it was too slow to catch its own food.

'Ultrasaurus'
(Ul-tra-saw-rus)

As this unofficial name suggests, 'Ultrasaurus' was truly enormous. Its fossils have only recently been found and scientists have not yet had time to study them properly. It seems that 'Ultrasaurus' was similar to Brachiosaurus, but it was even larger. It would have been 30 metres long, and tall enough to look over the top of a four-storey building. 'Ultrasaurus' may have been the largest animal ever to have lived on earth.

'Ultrasaurus'

Velociraptor

Velociraptor
(Vel-owe-sir-ap-tor)

This dinosaur was smaller than a man and lived in Mongolia 75 million years ago. It was a meat-eating dinosaur that attacked other animals with the sharp, hooked claws on its hind legs.

Ww-Yy-Zz

Wannanosaurus

— Wannanosaurus —
(Wan-an-owe-saw-rus)

Wannanosaurus lived in China during the Cretaceous period. Its name means 'reptile from Wannan'. It was a bone-headed dinosaur, like Stegoceras.

Yangchuanosaurus

— Yangchuanosaurus —
(Yan-chew-an-owe-saw-rus)

This powerful hunter lived 145 million years ago in China. It was nearly three times as long as a car and had strong legs. Yangchuanosaurus was a relative of Allosaurus and could probably run quickly. It would have been able to attack and eat large dinosaurs. Its fossil skeleton was discovered in 1978.

Zephyrosaurus

— Zephyrosaurus —
(Zeff-ear-owe-saw-rus)

This two-legged dinosaur lived 120 million years ago in North America. Zephyrosaurus meant 'the reptile of the wind'. It was 2 metres long and ate plants.